The Ultimate Cold Storage Wallet:

Seed Words, Key Phrases, & Password Storage

Lite

By Dennis B Cooper

This Book Belongs to

Name:______________________________

Address:____________________________

____

Phone:_____________________________

Email:_____________________________

With a Cash Reward Upon Return

$_____________

This publication is designed to provide competent and reliable information regarding the subject matter covered. It also contains the opinions and ideas of its author. However, it is sold with the understanding that the author and publisher are not engaged in rendering legal, tax, investment, financial, accounting, or other professional advice or services. Laws and practices often vary from state to state, and if legal or other expert assistance is required, the services of a professional should be sought. The authors and publisher specifically disclaim any liability incurred from the use or application of the contents of this book. No warranty is made with respect to the accuracy or completeness of the information contained herein, and both the author and the publisher specifically disclaim any responsibility for any liability, loss, or risk, personal or otherwise, which is incurred as a consequence, directly or indirectly, of the use and application of any of the contents of this book.

Table of Contents

Directions on How to Use Each Section

Password Keeper

Security is one of, if not the most, important part of holding cryptocurrency. Having someone gain access to your investments could lead to a massive loss of time, effort, and money on your part and could leave you in a financial mess you may not be able to come back from. So in this book, there are 40 spaces (5 pages) for 40 different websites, usernames, and passwords to keep track of bank accounts, investment accounts, cryptocurrency trading accounts, stock trading accounts, and any other security information you deem necessary. Having a secure place offline to keep this information will make it significantly harder for someone to get their hands on it.

Hot Wallet Seed Words

Here you have a few pages to list your hot wallet sites, your 8-digit PIN, and 13 spaces to write down your seed words. You are only given 12 words, so this 13th space is there to provide you with another level of security. You can add an obligatory word that only you know to the list that will be hard for anyone who may find this to gain access to your cryptocurrency, thus ensuring that a loved one is the only person to gain access to your cryptocurrency. Also, extra pages for multiple accounts or pages to use as fake pages to throw off someone.

Cold Wallet Seed Words

24 seed words are given to secure your hardware wallet, and just like with the hot wallet seed words, there is an extra space here to insert a word that will throw off any would-be thief. As well 6 pages for more than one

Hardware wallet or to make fake pages so the unscrupulous person who may find this won't be able to figure out the precautions you added.

Crypto/Stock Traders Log

Crypto/Stock _______________ Ticker symbol ___________
____

Date	Day your transaction takes place
Trading Platform	Place where you purchased from
Trade Type	Is it a short term, medium term, and long-term trade
Entry Price	Price you purchased units the currency
Quantity	How many your purchased
Total Cost	Total of all the purchased
Notes	The reason you purchased this Cryptocurrency or stock. The thoughts on your strategy for it. Anything you want to remind yourself you put into your notes column
Take Profit	What price you plan to sell to take a certain percentage of profit
Stop Loss	At what price do you plan to sell if it drops below a certain price point.
Closing Price	Price you sold out
Profit/loss	How much you profited/lost from the trade
Remarks/Comments transaction	To track your state of mind for this particular
Notes	The reasons these transactions either profited or lost and what you learned from the transactions so far.

Instructions in Case of Emergency

Creating a backup plan or instructions in case of your death are something most people overlook or deem a waste of time. But unfortunately, accidents happen, and things beyond our control can turn our lives upside-down. So, with the mindset of always being prepared, this section gives you a place to instruct whomever you bestow your stock and cryptocurrency investments to how to access your wallets and where they might find the secret keys to how you set up this book.

Hot Wallet Seed Words   Date:________

Website:______________________________

Username:____________________________

Password:____________________________

8 Digit PIN: _ _ _ _ _ _ _ _

		1
2	3	4
5	6	7
8	9	10
11	12	13

Notes:______________________________

Hot Wallet Seed Words Date:________

Website:______________________________

Username:_____________________________

Password:_____________________________

8 Digit PIN: _ _ _ _ _ _ _ _

		1
2	3	4
5	6	7
8	9	10
11	12	13

Notes:________________________________

____

____

____

____

____

____

Hot Wallet Seed Words Date:__________

Website:______________________________

Username:______________________________

Password:______________________________

8 Digit PIN: _ _ _ _ _ _ _ _

		1
2	3	4
5	6	7
8	9	10
11	12	13

Notes:______________________________

____

____

____

____

____

____

Hot Wallet Seed Words Date:________

Website:______________________________

Username:____________________________

Password:____________________________

8 Digit PIN: _ _ _ _ _ _ _ _

		1
2	3	4
5	6	7
8	9	10
11	12	13

Notes:______________________________

Hot Wallet Seed Words

Date:__________

Website:______________________________________

Username:____________________________________

Password:____________________________________

8 Digit PIN: _ _ _ _ _ _ _ _ _ _

		1
2	3	4
5	6	7
8	9	10
11	12	13

Notes:_______________________________________

____

____

____

____

____

____

Hot Wallet Seed Words   Date:________

Website:________________________________

Username:________________________________

Password:________________________________

8 Digit PIN: _ _ _ _ _ _ _ _

		1
2	3	4
5	6	7
8	9	10
11	12	13

Notes:________________________________

____

____

____

____

____

____

Cold Storage Seed Words Date:________

Password:________________________________

Wallet:______________________

		1
2	3	4
5	6	7
8	9	10
11	12	13
14	15	16
17	18	19
20	21	22
23	24	25

Notes:________________________________

____

Cold Storage Seed Words Date:________

Password:______________________________

Wallet:____________________

		1
2	3	4
5	6	7
8	9	10
11	12	13
14	15	16
17	18	19
20	21	22
23	24	25

Notes:______________________________

____

Cold Storage Seed Words Date:________

Password:______________________________

Wallet:____________________

		1
2	3	4
5	6	7
8	9	10
11	12	13
14	15	16
17	18	19
20	21	22
23	24	25

Notes:______________________________

____

Cold Storage Seed Words Date:________

Password:______________________________

Wallet:____________________

		1
2	3	4
5	6	7
8	9	10
11	12	13
14	15	16
17	18	19
20	21	22
23	24	25

Notes:______________________________

____

Cold Storage Seed Words Date:________

Password:______________________________

Wallet:______________________

		1
2	3	4
5	6	7
8	9	10
11	12	13
14	15	16
17	18	19
20	21	22
23	24	25

Notes:______________________________

____

Cold Storage Seed Words Date:________

Password:______________________________

Wallet:____________________

		1
2	3	4
5	6	7
8	9	10
11	12	13
14	15	16
17	18	19
20	21	22
23	24	25

Notes:______________________________

____

PASSWORD LOG

Site Name:	
Site Address:	
Login/username:	
Password:	

Site Name:	
Site Address:	
Login/username:	
Password:	

Site Name:	
Site Address:	
Login/username:	
Password:	

Site Name:	
Site Address:	
Login/username:	
Password:	

Site Name:	
Site Address:	
Login/username:	
Password:	

PASSWORD LOG

Site Name:	
Site Address:	
Login/username:	
Password:	

Site Name:	
Site Address:	
Login/username:	
Password:	

Site Name:	
Site Address:	
Login/username:	
Password:	

Site Name:	
Site Address:	
Login/username:	
Password:	

Site Name:	
Site Address:	
Login/username:	
Password:	

PASSWORD LOG

Site Name:	
Site Address:	
Login/username:	
Password:	

Site Name:	
Site Address:	
Login/username:	
Password:	

Site Name:	
Site Address:	
Login/username:	
Password:	

Site Name:	
Site Address:	
Login/username:	
Password:	

Site Name:	
Site Address:	
Login/username:	
Password:	

PASSWORD LOG

Site Name:	
Site Address:	
Login/username:	
Password:	

Site Name:	
Site Address:	
Login/username:	
Password:	

Site Name:	
Site Address:	
Login/username:	
Password:	

Site Name:	
Site Address:	
Login/username:	
Password:	

Site Name:	
Site Address:	
Login/username:	
Password:	

PASSWORD LOG

Site Name:
Site Address:
Login/username:
Password:

Site Name:
Site Address:
Login/username:
Password:

Site Name:
Site Address:
Login/username:
Password:

Site Name:
Site Address:
Login/username:
Password:

Site Name:
Site Address:
Login/username:
Password:

PASSWORD LOG

Site Name:
Site Address:
Login/username:
Password:

Site Name:
Site Address:
Login/username:
Password:

Site Name:
Site Address:
Login/username:
Password:

Site Name:
Site Address:
Login/username:
Password:

Site Name:
Site Address:
Login/username:
Password:

PASSWORD LOG

Site Name:	
Site Address:	
Login/username:	
Password:	

Site Name:	
Site Address:	
Login/username:	
Password:	

Site Name:	
Site Address:	
Login/username:	
Password:	

Site Name:	
Site Address:	
Login/username:	
Password:	

Site Name:	
Site Address:	
Login/username:	
Password:	

PASSWORD LOG

Site Name:
Site Address:
Login/username:
Password:

Site Name:
Site Address:
Login/username:
Password:

Site Name:
Site Address:
Login/username:
Password:

Site Name:
Site Address:
Login/username:
Password:

Site Name:
Site Address:
Login/username:
Password:

PASSWORD LOG

Site Name:	
Site Address:	
Login/username:	
Password:	

Site Name:	
Site Address:	
Login/username:	
Password:	

Site Name:	
Site Address:	
Login/username:	
Password:	

Site Name:	
Site Address:	
Login/username:	
Password:	

Site Name:	
Site Address:	
Login/username:	
Password:	

PASSWORD LOG

Site Name:	
Site Address:	
Login/username:	
Password:	

Site Name:	
Site Address:	
Login/username:	
Password:	

Site Name:	
Site Address:	
Login/username:	
Password:	

Site Name:	
Site Address:	
Login/username:	
Password:	

Site Name:	
Site Address:	
Login/username:	
Password:	

Crypto/Stock ________________ Ticker symbol___________

Date	Trading Platform	Trade Type	Entry Price	Quanity	Total Cost

Notes____

____

____

____

Crypto/Stock ________________ Ticker symbol ___________

Take Profit	Stop Loss	Closing Price	Profit/Loss	Comments

Notes ____

____

____

____

Crypto/Stock ________________ Ticker symbol___________

Date	Trading Platform	Trade Type	Entry Price	Quanity	Total Cost

Notes

Crypto/Stock ________________ Ticker symbol ___________

Take Profit	Stop Loss	Closing Price	Profit/Loss	Comments

Notes ____

____

____

____

Crypto/Stock ________________ Ticker symbol___________

Date	Trading Platform	Trade Type	Entry Price	Quanity	Total Cost

Notes____

____

____

____

Crypto/Stock ________________ Ticker symbol____________

Take Profit	Stop Loss	Closing Price	Profit/Loss	Comments

Notes____

____

____

____

Crypto/Stock ________________ Ticker symbol __________

Date	Trading Platform	Trade Type	Entry Price	Quanity	Total Cost

Notes ____

____

____

____

Crypto/Stock ______________ Ticker symbol __________

Take Profit	Stop Loss	Closing Price	Profit/Loss	Comments

Notes ____

____

____

____

Crypto/Stock ________________ Ticker symbol___________

Date	Trading Platform	Trade Type	Entry Price	Quanity	Total Cost

Notes____

____

____

____

Crypto/Stock ________________ Ticker symbol___________

Take Profit	Stop Loss	Closing Price	Profit/Loss	Comments

Notes____

____

____

____

Crypto/Stock ________________ Ticker symbol___________

Date	Trading Platform	Trade Type	Entry Price	Quanity	Total Cost

Notes____

____

____

____

Crypto/Stock ____________ Ticker symbol ________

Take Profit	Stop Loss	Closing Price	Profit/Loss	Comments

Notes ____

____

____

____

Crypto/Stock ________________ Ticker symbol ___________

Date	Trading Platform	Trade Type	Entry Price	Quanity	Total Cost

Notes ____

____

____

____

Crypto/Stock ________________ Ticker symbol___________

Take Profit	Stop Loss	Closing Price	Profit/Loss	Comments

Notes____

____

____

____

Crypto/Stock ________________ Ticker symbol___________

Date	Trading Platform	Trade Type	Entry Price	Quanity	Total Cost

Notes____

____

____

____

Crypto/Stock ________________ Ticker symbol ___________

Take Profit	Stop Loss	Closing Price	Profit/Loss	Comments

Notes ____

____

____

____

Crypto/Stock ________________ Ticker symbol ___________

Date	Trading Platform	Trade Type	Entry Price	Quanity	Total Cost

Notes ____

____

____

____

Crypto/Stock ______________ Ticker symbol__________

Take Profit	Stop Loss	Closing Price	Profit/Loss	Comments

Notes____

____

____

____

Crypto/Stock ________________ Ticker symbol ___________

Date	Trading Platform	Trade Type	Entry Price	Quanity	Total Cost

Notes ____

____

____

____

Crypto/Stock ________________ Ticker symbol___________

Take Profit	Stop Loss	Closing Price	Profit/Loss	Comments

Notes____

____

____

____

Crypto/Stock ________________ Ticker symbol ___________

Date	Trading Platform	Trade Type	Entry Price	Quanity	Total Cost

Notes ____

____

____

____

Crypto/Stock ________________ Ticker symbol ____________

Take Profit	Stop Loss	Closing Price	Profit/Loss	Comments

Notes ____

____

____

____

Crypto/Stock ________________ Ticker symbol ____________

Date	Trading Platform	Trade Type	Entry Price	Quanity	Total Cost

Notes ____

____

____

____

Crypto/Stock ________________ Ticker symbol __________

Take Profit	Stop Loss	Closing Price	Profit/Loss	Comments

Notes ____

____

____

____

Crypto/Stock ________________ Ticker symbol ___________

Date	Trading Platform	Trade Type	Entry Price	Quanity	Total Cost

Notes ____

____

____

____

Crypto/Stock ______________ Ticker symbol __________

Take Profit	Stop Loss	Closing Price	Profit/Loss	Comments

Notes ____

____

____

____

Crypto/Stock ________________ Ticker symbol___________

Date	Trading Platform	Trade Type	Entry Price	Quanity	Total Cost

Notes____

____

____

____

Crypto/Stock ________________ Ticker symbol ___________

Take Profit	Stop Loss	Closing Price	Profit/Loss	Comments

Notes ____

____

____

____

Crypto/Stock ________________ Ticker symbol___________

Date	Trading Platform	Trade Type	Entry Price	Quanity	Total Cost

Notes____

____

____

____

Crypto/Stock ________________ Ticker symbol ___________

Take Profit	Stop Loss	Closing Price	Profit/Loss	Comments

Notes ____

____

____

____

Crypto/Stock ________________ Ticker symbol ___________

Date	Trading Platform	Trade Type	Entry Price	Quanity	Total Cost

Notes ____

____

____

____

Crypto/Stock ________________ Ticker symbol___________

Take Profit	Stop Loss	Closing Price	Profit/Loss	Comments

Notes____

____

____

____

Crypto/Stock ________________ Ticker symbol__________

Date	Trading Platform	Trade Type	Entry Price	Quanity	Total Cost

Notes____

____

____

____

Crypto/Stock ______________ Ticker symbol __________

Take Profit	Stop Loss	Closing Price	Profit/Loss	Comments

Notes ____

____

____

____

Crypto/Stock ________________ Ticker symbol___________

Date	Trading Platform	Trade Type	Entry Price	Quanity	Total Cost

Notes____

____

____

____

Crypto/Stock ________________ Ticker symbol ___________

Take Profit	Stop Loss	Closing Price	Profit/Loss	Comments

Notes ____

____

____

____

Crypto/Stock ____________ Ticker symbol ____________

Date	Trading Platform	Trade Type	Entry Price	Quanity	Total Cost

Notes ____

____

____

____

Crypto/Stock ______________ Ticker symbol __________

Take Profit	Stop Loss	Closing Price	Profit/Loss	Comments

Notes ____

____

____

____

Crypto/Stock ________________ Ticker symbol___________

Date	Trading Platform	Trade Type	Entry Price	Quanity	Total Cost

Notes____

____

____

____

Crypto/Stock ________________ Ticker symbol___________

Take Profit	Stop Loss	Closing Price	Profit/Loss	Comments

Notes____

____

____

____

Crypto/Stock ____________ Ticker symbol ____________

Date	Trading Platform	Trade Type	Entry Price	Quanity	Total Cost

Notes ____

Crypto/Stock ______________ Ticker symbol __________

Take Profit	Stop Loss	Closing Price	Profit/Loss	Comments

Notes ____

Crypto/Stock ________________ Ticker symbol ___________

Date	Trading Platform	Trade Type	Entry Price	Quanity	Total Cost

Notes ____

____

____

____

Crypto/Stock ______________ Ticker symbol __________

Take Profit	Stop Loss	Closing Price	Profit/Loss	Comments

Notes ____

____

____

____

Crypto/Stock ________________ Ticker symbol ___________

Date	Trading Platform	Trade Type	Entry Price	Quanity	Total Cost

Notes ____

____

____

____

Crypto/Stock ________________ Ticker symbol___________

Take Profit	Stop Loss	Closing Price	Profit/Loss	Comments

Notes____

____

____

____

Crypto/Stock ________________ Ticker symbol___________

Date	Trading Platform	Trade Type	Entry Price	Quanity	Total Cost

Notes____

____

____

____

Crypto/Stock ________________ Ticker symbol ___________

Take Profit	Stop Loss	Closing Price	Profit/Loss	Comments

Notes ____

____

____

____

Crypto/Stock ________________ Ticker symbol ___________

Date	Trading Platform	Trade Type	Entry Price	Quanity	Total Cost

Notes ____

____

____

____

Crypto/Stock ________________ Ticker symbol___________

Take Profit	Stop Loss	Closing Price	Profit/Loss	Comments

Notes____

____

____

____

Crypto/Stock ________________ Ticker symbol ___________

Date	Trading Platform	Trade Type	Entry Price	Quanity	Total Cost

Notes ____

____

____

____

Crypto/Stock ______________ Ticker symbol __________

Take Profit	Stop Loss	Closing Price	Profit/Loss	Comments

Notes ____

____

____

____

Crypto/Stock ________________ Ticker symbol___________

Date	Trading Platform	Trade Type	Entry Price	Quanity	Total Cost

Notes____

____

____

____

Crypto/Stock ________________ Ticker symbol ___________

Take Profit	Stop Loss	Closing Price	Profit/Loss	Comments

Notes ____

____

____

____

Crypto/Stock ________________ Ticker symbol ___________

Date	Trading Platform	Trade Type	Entry Price	Quanity	Total Cost

Notes____

____

____

____

Crypto/Stock ______________ Ticker symbol__________

Take Profit	Stop Loss	Closing Price	Profit/Loss	Comments

Notes____

____

____

____

Crypto/Stock ________________ Ticker symbol ___________

Date	Trading Platform	Trade Type	Entry Price	Quanity	Total Cost

Notes ____

____

____

____

Crypto/Stock ________________ Ticker symbol ___________

Take Profit	Stop Loss	Closing Price	Profit/Loss	Comments

Notes ____

____

____

____

Crypto/Stock ________________ Ticker symbol ___________

Date	Trading Platform	Trade Type	Entry Price	Quanity	Total Cost

Notes ____

____

____

____

Crypto/Stock ______________ Ticker symbol __________

Take Profit	Stop Loss	Closing Price	Profit/Loss	Comments

Notes ____

Crypto/Stock ________________ Ticker symbol ___________

Date	Trading Platform	Trade Type	Entry Price	Quanity	Total Cost

Notes ____

____

____

____

Crypto/Stock ______________ Ticker symbol__________

Take Profit	Stop Loss	Closing Price	Profit/Loss	Comments

Notes ____

____

____

____

Crypto/Stock ________________ Ticker symbol ____________

Date	Trading Platform	Trade Type	Entry Price	Quanity	Total Cost

Notes ____

____

____

____

Crypto/Stock ________________ Ticker symbol____________

Take Profit	Stop Loss	Closing Price	Profit/Loss	Comments

Notes____

____

____

____

Crypto/Stock ________________ Ticker symbol___________

Date	Trading Platform	Trade Type	Entry Price	Quanity	Total Cost

Notes____

____

____

____

Crypto/Stock ________________ Ticker symbol ___________

Take Profit	Stop Loss	Closing Price	Profit/Loss	Comments

Notes ____

____

____

____

Crypto/Stock ________________ Ticker symbol ___________

Date	Trading Platform	Trade Type	Entry Price	Quanity	Total Cost

Notes ____

____

____

____

Crypto/Stock ______________ Ticker symbol __________

Take Profit	Stop Loss	Closing Price	Profit/Loss	Comments

Notes ____

____

____

____

Crypto/Stock ________________ Ticker symbol ___________

Date	Trading Platform	Trade Type	Entry Price	Quanity	Total Cost

Notes ____

____

____

____

Crypto/Stock ________________ Ticker symbol___________

Take Profit	Stop Loss	Closing Price	Profit/Loss	Comments

Notes____

____

____

____

Crypto/Stock ________________ Ticker symbol___________

Date	Trading Platform	Trade Type	Entry Price	Quanity	Total Cost

Notes____

____

____

____

Crypto/Stock ________________ Ticker symbol ____________

Take Profit	Stop Loss	Closing Price	Profit/Loss	Comments

Notes ____

____

____

____

Crypto/Stock ________________ Ticker symbol ___________

Date	Trading Platform	Trade Type	Entry Price	Quanity	Total Cost

Notes ____

____

____

____

Crypto/Stock ________________ Ticker symbol___________

Take Profit	Stop Loss	Closing Price	Profit/Loss	Comments

Notes____

____

____

____

Crypto/Stock ________________ Ticker symbol ___________

Date	Trading Platform	Trade Type	Entry Price	Quanity	Total Cost

Notes ____

____

____

____

Crypto/Stock ________________ Ticker symbol___________

Take Profit	Stop Loss	Closing Price	Profit/Loss	Comments

Notes____

____

____

____

Crypto/Stock ________________ Ticker symbol___________

Date	Trading Platform	Trade Type	Entry Price	Quanity	Total Cost

Notes____

____

____

____

Crypto/Stock ________________ Ticker symbol____________

Take Profit	Stop Loss	Closing Price	Profit/Loss	Comments

Notes____

____

____

____

In Case of Emergency Instructions